W9-ADC-118

EXPLORE LIFE CYCLES

A Frog's Life Cycle

by Mary R. Dunn

CAPSTONE PRESS
a capstone imprint

Pebble Plus is published by Capstone Press,
1710 Roe Crest Drive, North Mankato, Minnesota 56003
www.mycapstone.com

Library of Congress Cataloging-in-Publication Data
Library of Congress Cataloging-in-Publication data is available on the Library of Congress website.
ISBN 978-1-5157-7052-7 (library binding)
ISBN 978-1-5157-7058-9 (paperback)
ISBN 978-1-5157-7064-0 (eBook PDF)

Editorial Credits
Anna Butzer, editor; Kyle Grenz, designer
Wanda Winch, media researcher; Kathy McColley, production specialist

Photo Credits
© Dwight Kuhn - all Rights Reserved, 13; Newscom: Photoshot/NHPA/Thomas Kitchin & Victoria Hurst, 11, 15; Science Source: ER Degginger, 9; Shutterstock: Astrid Gast, 7, Chris Hill, 1, Eivaisla, back cover, Jacques Durocher, 5, Jason Patrick Ross, 19, Jay Ondreicka, cover, 21, Tristan tan, frog silhouettes; Thinkstock: iStockphoto/SteveByland, 17

Note to Parents and Teachers

The Explore Life Cycles set supports national science standards related to life science. This book describes and illustrates the life cycle of wood frogs. The images support early readers in understanding the text. The repetition of words and phrases helps early readers learn new words. This book also introduces early readers to subject-specific vocabulary words, which are defined in the Glossary section. Early readers may need assistance to read some words and to use the Table of Contents, Glossary, Read More, Internet Sites, Critical Thinking Questions, and Index sections of the book.

Printed and bound in China.
010408F17

Table of Contents

Eggs in the Pond

Many kinds of frogs live around the world. Frogs are amphibians. They can live in water and on land. All frogs have the same life cycle.

Wood frogs live in wetlands.
In spring, females lay eggs
in water. A thick, clear jelly holds
the eggs together. Tadpoles grow inside.

Growing Tadpoles

Tadpoles hatch from the eggs
in about 14 days. Using their
long tails, they swim around the pond.
Tadpoles eat algae and grow fast.

A tadpole's body goes through many changes. First, it grows back legs. Then lungs take the place of gills. The tadpole can now breathe out of water.

Next, the tadpole begins to grow front legs. Its tail gets shorter and shorter.

The tadpole becomes a froglet.

Frisky Froglets

A froglet spends time in water and on land. It uses its new legs to search for food. The froglet hops in the woods looking for insects.

After about four months
a froglet fully loses its tail.
It becomes an adult frog.
Wood frogs live for three to four years.

Adult Frogs

Adult wood frogs are tan or brown.
In the fall they crawl under leaves.
During winter, frogs freeze as hard
as ice cubes. Their hearts stop beating.

In spring, wood frogs thaw.

They hop into ponds.

Males croak mating calls to females.

The life cycle of a frog begins again.

GLOSSARY

algae—small plants without roots or stems that grow in water

amphibian—an animal that lives on water and on land

freeze—to become solid or icy at a very low temperature

froglet—a tiny frog that has recently developed from a tadpole

gill—body part used to breathe underwater

lung—body part used to breathe air

mate—to join together to produce young

thaw—to become unfrozen

READ MORE

De la Bedoyere, Camille. *Tadpole to Frog.* Life Cycles. Beverly, Mass.: QEB Publishing, 2016.

Jones, Grace. *Life Cycle of a Frog.* Hardwick, UK: Booklife, 2016.

Pfeffer, Wendy. *From Tadpole to Frog.* New York: Harper Collins, 2015.

Zemlicka, Shannon. *From Tadpole to Frog.* Minneapolis: Lerner Publications, 2012.

INTERNET SITES

FactHound offers a safe, fun way to find Internet sites related to this book. All of the sites on FactHound have been researched by our staff.

Here's all you do:

Visit *www.facthound.com*

Type in this code: 9781515770527

CRITICAL THINKING QUESTIONS

1. Why are dead leaves a good place for wood frogs to stay in fall and winter?
2. Find the words "lungs" and "gills" in the glossary. How are both important to wood frogs?
3. What are the favorite foods of tadpoles and frogs?

INDEX